Spirit of the Bedroom

Spirit of the Bedroom

Jane Alexander

WATSON-GUPTILL PUBLICATIONS/NEW YORK

First published in the United States in 2002 by
Watson-Guptill Publications
a division of VNU Business Media, Inc.
770 Broadway, New York, New York 10003
www.watsonguptill.com

First published in the UK in 2002 by Element
An imprint of HarperCollins*Publishers*
77-85 Fulham Palace Road
Hammersmith, London W6 8JB

1 2 3 4 5 6 / 07 06 05 04 03 02

Jane Alexander asserts the moral right
to be identified as the author of this work
Editor: Jillian Stewart
Design: Wheelhouse Creative
Production: Melanie Vandevelde

Library of Congress Control Number: 2001119258

ISBN: 0 8230 4900 0

Printed and bound in Hong Kong

Contents

Introduction

A bedroom, with its links to sleep and dreams, intimacy or aloneness, is one of the most beguiling and mysterious rooms in the home. The bedroom is the first room we see each morning and the last space we see at night—it closes the circle of our waking life. It's a place which has to hold us through the night and keep us while we dream. Bedrooms are personal, highly personal. This is the room in which we are most likely to make love, to fantasize, to encounter our sensuality—to meet another human being at the most intimate level. But a good bedroom is also a solitary sanctuary, a place outside the hubbub of the house, a *tenemos* of private dreams and deep nurturing of the soul. With its domination over the unconscious part of our lives, you might argue the bedroom is the most important room in the entire home.

Yet, despite its importance, the bedroom is often neglected. We pay more practical attention to the "public" rooms of the house—those which our visitors will see, those which hold court over the waking hours. The bedroom gets pushed to the back. Hopefully this little book will encourage you to look on your bedroom in a whole new light.

Personally, my bedroom is probably my favorite room in the entire house. It's the room in which I am entirely myself. It faces east so in the morning the sun pours in through the windows and at night I can track the moon on the first half of its journey. House martins nest under the eaves and as I write this I watch their darting, swooping returns— so fast you think they are going to crash into our windows.

I've kept the décor calm. The walls are a warm cream and the carpet a slightly darker mushroom. Slatted wooden blinds filter the light, creating a dappled effect. Bright duvet covers and soft throws and cushions provide splashes of color, depending on my mood. It's a calm, uncluttered space yet by no means minimal.

Next to my side of the bed is a small bookcase with my most favorite books for dipping into before sleep and on waking. My collection of goddesses gaze rather sternly from the mantelpiece and three small altars sit on the window ledges filled with my "soul" objects of the moment.

Curiously I find that the bedroom is a place in which I can fulfill my three major roles in life quite smoothly and without competition. I tend to go to bed before my husband and this early part of the night is "me" time. When the bedside lights are on the room is bathed in a soft light and feels like a welcoming cocoon. I often find myself sneaking off early so I can sit and revel in the peace after a long day balancing work and the demands of a small child. I am alone in the nicest possible way. In archetypal terms, it's my Artemis time—wild, solitary, self-possessed, shy of company.

But light the many scented candles and it becomes a sensual retreat, a place of intimacy and closeness, of warmth and tenderness. Aphrodite comes out to play and the bedroom shifts focus.

Come morning, a small child squirrels himself into the middle of the bed and we all snooze companionably as the world comes to life outside. The bed becomes a ship, a space-craft, a nomad's tent, a cave. We share books and tell tales: it's precious bonding time before the onslaught of another hectic day. I find myself as Demeter, motherly and warm, embracing my family and reveling in their comfort.

These are my thoughts of bedroom. Yours will probably be quite different. But hopefully already you will be thinking about what you need and want from *your* bedroom. Over the pages that follow we'll look at how you might discover—and achieve—your desires.

First Steps

Bedrooms need a lot of musing, a lot of dreaming. So don't race in and get painting, or shifting furniture. Spend some time first of all in quiet pondering. Let your mind range around and allow your unconscious to come up with curious and unusual ideas. Here are some introductory and highly practical ways to help you if you're not familiar with this process.

Your ideal bedroom

Spend some time looking through magazines (virtually every magazine and supplement now has a home section, quite apart from the huge number of dedicated homes magazines). Clip out pictures of bedrooms (or other rooms) that really appeal to you. Also cut out pictures which relay the kind of feeling you want from your room—this could be anything: a beautiful sunset across a deserted beach, a tangle of limbs as children invade the family bed, a minimalist-style restaurant, dappled light in a cool forest, or a hot steamy sex scene. Let your imagination run riot.

You may find some interesting concepts emerge. Perhaps you have always

dreamed of a huge baronial bedroom yet the pictures you have chosen show cosy, intimate spaces. Maybe you think you like cool minimalism but, if so, what are all these sumptuous velvets and tons of pillows and cushions doing rampaging over your clipped-out pictures? Our subconscious mind works in images so this is a powerful way to discover what your inner mind and soul really wants from a bedroom.

Now make your bedroom "treasure map." Take a large sheet of paper and put your very favorite images on it. Add a picture of yourself and anyone with whom you share your bedroom. Leave it somewhere you can see it every day and note your responses. You may well find that over a period of days or weeks your views change. If you do share your bedroom it can be a great idea to have your partner (or whoever) do a treasure

map too. Do them separately and make a commitment not to discuss them until they have been up for at least two weeks. Then sit down and debate your desires—you may well find that you have more in common than you anticipated.

Having decided on what you want, you can think about how you might introduce these elements into your own space. The key here is always to come back to the *feeling* you want. O.K, you may not live in

a baronial castle or a country cottage but what is it you like about these kinds of places? What feeling do they evoke? What mood? If it's something like "cosy, intimate, friendly, and warm" you can reproduce that feeling in a high-rise apartment with a little imagination. If you crave cool and spacious but have a tiny room you can still give a feeling of expansiveness by using color and furnishings cleverly.

Whose space is it?

Another interesting exercise is to draw out a rough map of your bedroom. It need not be draughtsman quality but should be pretty much to scale. Mark in pieces of furniture. Now pick a color for everyone who uses this room (i.e. yourself, your partner, possibly a baby or children who might invade from time to time). Color-in the parts of the room used by each person (you can have stripes if any parts are equally used; if one person dominates though, color it with their color). This allows you to see who is actually taking up space in your bedroom. It can be very illuminating. You might think it's your shared room so how come your partner has his desk in there and his piles of paper under the bed? How come half your wardrobe is taken up by your teenage daughter's clothes?

What are all these toy boxes doing in here? This isn't to say any of these things are wrong—but the exercise gives you the opportunity to figure out what's going on, and whether it works for you. Having a box of toys to keep an early riser amused is a pretty good idea—but maybe he or she could be persuaded it's more fun to play in their own room? Or maybe the garish plastic toy box could be moved out and a rather lovely painted chest brought in instead so your room looks like a bedroom instead of a crèche.

It's a good idea for everyone who uses the room to do one of these maps—you might find your impressions are totally different. Have a discussion—a friendly one (I always find a bottle of wine helps the process, but coffee and cake is another fine option).

A clean, clear space

Whatever you decide and whatever style of bedroom you desire, at base it needs to be an oasis of calm, offering a space in which to sleep and dream. Above all else, it needs to be devoid of the insidious clutter which seems to permeate all but the most minimalist of households. The first major practical step you can make to rejuvenate and restore your bedroom is to clear out all the mess. There is no "correct" method of doing it. You can be wimpish and do a drawer or closet a week or just plunge in with a pile of trash bags and clear the whole lot in one fell swoop.

Take a long hard look at your bedroom and identify all the problem areas. Some will stand out like sore thumbs. But it's not a case of "out of sight, out of mind," you need to go beyond cosmetic anti-clutter

and check all those hidden places too: in your closets and cupboards; drawers and dressers; and, yes, under the bed! There's no point having an immaculate bedroom when every time you open the closet door you're confronted by chaos. Most of the time it isn't noticeable on a physical level but psychologically it's still clutter and, however subconsciously, you know it's there and it's affecting you.

Here's a quick check-list of what to do with all that stuff:

- Clothes. Do they fit you (now, not in some hypothetical future)? Do they suit you? Do you actually like them? If not, give them to a charity store.
- Cosmetics and perfumes. These don't last indefinitely so chuck out anything that has been languishing for over a year or so.
- Books, CDs. Don't overload your bedroom with books and hi-fi stuff. If you don't re-read your books give them to book exchanges or friends.
- Letters and papers, cards and mementos. Select the ones you really want to keep and store or display them in attractive boxes or files (cover them with pretty paper or fabric so they look nice). Try to remember that life is for living now, not for reliving yesterday.
- Ornaments and knick-knacks. Somehow we seem to accumulate little bits and pieces in bedrooms. If it's been given to you and you hate it, let it go. I find the odd white lie (i.e. "it fell and broke") useful here if challenged on the absence of a horrible gift.
- Other people's stuff. It's even more vexing if it's not even your stuff which is clogging your room. Give the offenders a certain amount of time (a couple of hours? A weekend?) to claim any belongings they really want. After that, out they go. Playgroups and nursery schools might be grateful for any old toys and games. Clothes might be welcomed at a women's refuge or a center for the homeless.
- Magazines. It's strange how magazines multiply. Don't hang onto magazines for years. Either pass them round among friends when you've read them or snip out your favorite pictures and put together a journal of inspiring images for future reference.

Feng Shui Fundamentals

Feng shui, often dubbed "acupuncture for houses," has become wildly popular in recent years. At first the idea sounds crazy: how can shifting your furniture change your luck? How can moving a mirror bring in more money? Why does it matter if there is a beam over your bed? It all sounds insane. However, if you can believe that our homes are full of subtle energy, constantly moving, then it makes sense that the layout of our rooms, the positioning of our furniture and other features, can affect how that energy flows.

What is feng shui?

If you're new to all this, let's recap a little. Feng shui evolved around five thousand years ago in China. The ancient Chinese believed that invisible life energy (called *chi* or *qi*) flowed through everything in life. It's the same philosophy that underlies acupuncture. If the energy in your body is flowing freely and easily, you will stay fit and healthy. If, however, the energy becomes stagnant or blocked, or erratic and undisciplined (through bad diet and lifestyle or weakness in an organ) you will most likely fall ill. The needles of acupuncture simply act by removing the blockages or calming the energy flow—they regulate the qi. The principle is exactly the same in houses. The Chinese believed that the buildings we live in require as much attention as our bodies and so developed this highly complex science for "healing" the environment. Centuries of observation showed that different areas of the house and different parts of each room attracted specific energies. Furthermore they discovered that certain configurations (the layout of rooms or even the position of furniture or features) could either help or hinder the free, smooth flowing of energy. At its core, feng shui teaches that by making small changes to your home you can affect everything in your life, from your finances to your health, from your relationships to your spirituality.

14 ... spirit of the bedroom

The Ba-gua

At the heart of feng shui lies the ba-gua. This is an octagonal template which divides any space (your entire home or simply a room within it) into eight areas. These eight areas (or corners) represent wealth (finances in general), fame (how you appear to the outside world), marriage (and all close relationships), children (and creativity), helpful people, career, knowledge (wisdom, inner knowing, spirituality), and the family (and your ancestors).

Different practitioners of feng shui use the ba-gua in different ways. However, all the feng shui consultants I have met so far use the following format which is, to my mind, also the most straightforward to learn. If you already know a fair amount about feng shui and are already using another method, stick with that by all means.

To work out the ba-gua of any room or house, the position of the main door is important. Imagine yourself standing with your back to the door: depending on the position of the main door you will be standing in either the knowledge, career, or helpful people corner of the ba-gua. Now envisage the ba-gua laid over your space. The wealth corner will be off in the far-left hand corner, the marriage corner in the far right-hand corner. You may find it easier to draw a map of your home and sketch the ba-gua over it, giving you an immediate idea of which corner lies in which room.

You can apply the ba-gua to any building or room, as illustrated on the following pages.

First of all, map your entire apartment or house. In which area does your bedroom fall? In an ideal world you

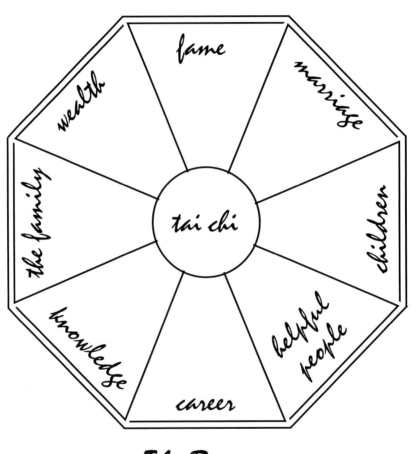

The Bagua

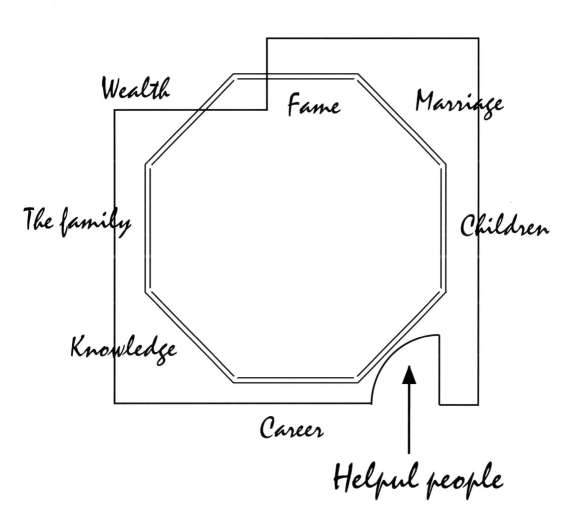

Wealth

Fame

Marriage

The family

Children

Knowledge

Career

Helpul people

would place your bedroom in the relationships corner (if you are either in a relationship or want to be in one). If you cannot have your bedroom in the best spot in your house, don't worry—you can often shift your bed and create equally good results.

So go into your bedroom and stand on the threshold with your back to the door. Depending on where your door lies you will be standing in either the Career area (the center), Helpful People (right-hand corner), or Knowledge (left-hand corner). Now you can plot the rest of the ba-gua—Wealth is in the far left-hand corner and Marriage in the far right-hand corner. Where you place your bed will depend on the age and circumstances of the person sleeping there.

- Children should always sleep in the Children position of the room. If the bed cannot be put there, put a lamp there plus something white (flowers or a fluffy toy perhaps). Keep colors soft for babies and very young children. For more ideas see the companion book to this *Spirit of the Nursery*.

- Fifteen to twenty-two year olds need plenty of peace and stability in their bedrooms. Their bed should be in the Knowledge position or, if this is impossible, put something black, blue, or green there. A plant, wind chime, or crystal could also help to boost that area. Books near the entrance to the room can help their studies.

- If you're in a relationship (and particularly if you're looking for one) you should make sure your bed is in the Marriage position. If that is impossible, put something red in that spot—maybe some rich velvet cushions or pillows or a sumptuous crimson throw. The shape of your bed is important too: while beds with separate mattresses may be supremely

comfortable, they could be divisive. Equally, twin beds could make relationships rocky.

- If you're seeking to get pregnant (or are already pregnant) you should neither move your bed nor dust underneath it. This is because according to the Chinese view of conception and birth the universe is full of spirits waiting to be born (known as *ling*). The *ling* are said to float under beds, waiting for the moment to enter the womb. If the bed is always being moved or cleaned, the *ling* might scatter, causing infertility or possibly even miscarriage.
- Older people should ideally sleep in the Family position. Again, if that's

impossible or difficult there is an alternative: put something green (or a plant, a wind chime, or crystal) in either the Wealth or Fame corners.

Other feng shui tips

There are a few other pointers for bedrooms.

- Beams look attractive but can symbolize division and ill-health in feng shui. If you have a beam directly above your bed running vertically down the bed it could cause problems in your relationship. If the beam cuts across your body horizontally, it could cause health problems—someone whose bed was in such a position that a beam cut across their throat had constant sore throats and tonsillitis.

- Built-in cupboards or shelves around or over the bed are awkward too, causing headaches, sore throats, and a feeling of being hemmed in. Keep the head of your bed as clear as possible and move beds away from beams. If that is impossible, drape the beam with garlands of dried hops (they'll give you sweet dreams too) or pin soft fabric along the beam to soften the energy shooting down onto you.

- Bedside cabinets, and bedroom furniture in general, should be soft and rounded. Avoid sharp corners and angular shapes. Mirrors are not a great idea in bedrooms and they should certainly not face your bed. They can cause insomnia or nightmares.

- Your bed should give you a clear view of the door. The ideal position for a bed is one where you can see the door clearly from your bed but not have it directly in front of you (i.e. with your feet pointing out the door). It may take some serious juggling to manage this and have your bed in the most auspicious position for your age and circumstances. If you can't do it, go with your intuition. Where does the bed feel right? Try it and see. If you don't sleep well in that position, ten to one you've picked a lousy spot. Shift it and try again (if you live in an apartment, take peace offerings to your neighbors!).

- Look through your windows and check the view. If you have a road coming directly at your home or if you have a church or large building in sight of your bedroom window, put up either a small silver ball (one of the Mayan bell balls is great) on a red string or a ba-gua mirror in the window.

Space Clearing

Every room, however large or small, is far more than walls, roof, floor, and furniture. These factors generally stay put but the subtle energy of the room is permanently shifting, moving, changing. In China (as we learned in the last chapter) this energy is known as *chi*, or *qi*. In India it is recognized as *prana*. The Japanese call it *ki*, and in the Middle East it is known as *qawa*. These ancient cultures have known for millennia what modern physics is only just discovering: that everything around us, whether it's a tree, a dog, or the kitchen table, is made up of energy. While the science remains mind-bogglingly baffling for most of us, we can all understand the theory in practice. If you've had a terrible argument, the room seems heavy and tense. We use the phrase "you could cut the air with a knife." The mood during a lively party is different again.

Ancient traditions

In cultures where this concept of vital energy is understood, people spend as much time on psychic clearing as they do

with their physical clearing. Unfortunately, in our technological societies, space clearing comes low down on our list of priorities. In fact it's safe to say that few Western homes will have ever been space cleared.

Imagine you hadn't physically cleaned your bedroom for ten years. No dusting, no vacuuming, no window cleaning— nothing. Imagine what it would look and feel like. It's a pretty unpleasant thought, isn't it? Now think about what has gone on in that room over the last ten years? You may have had lovely times there but equally you might have had rows, sat sobbing your heart out, felt depressed, or angry, or hopeless. Other people might have brought their negative feelings into that room. And what about the people who lived there before you? How do you know what energy they left behind them? Now realize that you've covered only the last ten years. If you are living in an old

building you could have decades, even centuries of hate, fear, loathing, malice, sadness, jealousy, resentment, and so forth built up like layers of grime. Of course you might be lucky and have happy, loving, joyous feelings sticking to the walls, but, even so, it's much better to start afresh and build up your own personal psychic atmosphere. The technique is pretty simple and is known as space clearing.

Preparing for space clearing

Although space clearing is generally totally safe there are several guidelines you should follow before clearing your home.

- Don't perform space clearing if you feel scared or apprehensive. If you feel a room has any kind of evil presence then you should seek out a trained professional (contact your local church or psychic center). Most of the energy in homes is just stuck or stale but some places do seem to have something heavier—call it a ghost, spirit, whatever—and you shouldn't try to shift that by yourself.

- Choose a time for space clearing when you feel fit, healthy, and emotionally balanced. It is also better not to perform space clearing when pregnant or menstruating as these are times when your energy should be turned within rather than without.
- Before you space clear, ensure you have carried out all your de-cluttering and have given the room a good physical spring-clean.
- Spend time thinking about what you want to achieve with your space clearing. Look back at your treasure map and try to encapsulate your

desires into one or two sentences of clear intent such as "My bedroom is a place of gentle serenity which embraces me with feelings of warmth, security, and tenderness." Or alternatively "I want my bedroom to be a raunchy love-nest!" How you put it is up to you but be clear in your mind about your intentions.

- Before you start work, have a shower or bath (you could use a few drops of a purifying oil such as lavender, juniper, or rosemary), wash your hair, and brush your teeth. Put on clean, fresh comfortable clothes. Remove all jewelry and your watch and avoid metal belts and buckles.
- If the weather is warm, it's best to be barefoot for space clearing. However, if you're space clearing in a cold house you can wear cotton socks or leather-soled slippers.

Space clearing ritual

Now let's move onto the clearing itself.

1 Take some time first of all to center yourself. Breathe deeply and evenly and allow yourself to feel calm and balanced. Visualize yourself surrounded by your aura, an egg-shaped cocoon filled with soft white light. Now expand that light to fill the whole of your bedroom. If it feels more natural, choose another color: some people like to imagine pure blue light, a soft rosy pink, gold, or golden pink.

2 Now starting at the main entrance to your room, hold your hand a few inches away from the wall and start to "sense" the energy. You should find, after a little practice, this comes quite easily. Your palm should face towards

the wall, with your hand parallel with your shoulder. The motion is similar to stroking a cat. You may find as you do this that you begin to get impressions. Work around your room, picking up feelings, sensing for "dull" or "stuck" spots where the energy feels sluggish. These areas will need most attention later.

3 Now choose a way to get in touch with the spirit or spirits of your bedroom. You may already be on good terms and know what they like. If not, the traditional ways to please the spirits are to light candles, burn incense, bring in flowers, and offer prayers. What you choose is up to you and your beliefs. But put your whole intention into whatever you choose. Put an offering on an altar (see page 86) or somewhere central. An ideal offering is one which uses all the

elements: flowers for earth, incense for air, a candle for fire, and a bowl of pure water for, obviously, water.

4 Clapping. The basic move of space clearing is clapping. Move steadily around the room systematically clapping into every corner, nook, and cranny. It sounds so simple but this is all it takes: you clap your hands into the corner, starting low and swiftly clapping on up towards the ceiling as high as you can. Repeat this as many times as necessary. You will know when you've clapped the corner clear because the sound of your clapping will become clearer. If you're still not sure, check the energy of the corner with your outstretched hand. As you clap imagine that your clapping is dispersing all the stagnant energy. That's it—now you just have to go around your whole space.

5 When you have finished your clapping, wash your hands thoroughly under running water.

6 Most professional space clearers would now use a bell. If you have a bell with a really pure clear tone, use that. Simply walk around the room again, this time ringing the bell as you go along. Your aim is to create a continuous circle of sound, so you need to ring the bell again before the last tone has died away. When you get back to your starting point, draw a horizontal figure of eight in the air with your bell. If you don't have a bell, don't worry—you will have done some serious cleansing with your clapping alone.

7 You may also like to use some of the new space clearing sprays which have come onto the market. I find these work best when combined with the traditional space clearing methods described above. They leave a lovely scent and can add an extra dimension to the work. For bedrooms I would recommend Angel Rejuvenation by Star Flower Essences, Sanctuary by Findhorn Flower Essences, or Heart Spirit by Pacific Essences (see the Resources section).

8 Finally you need to seal your newly energized and clean bedroom. Now go to the center of the room and fill the space once again with your expanded aura, imagining any remaining stagnant energy being pushed clean out of the room. Now you should shield the space. Stand at each corner of your room and imagine yourself bringing down a force-field of energy with a downwards sweep of your arm. The four fields merge together and create a safe haven, protecting you and your space.

The Healthy Bedroom

Although it may not seem like it, you are well on the way to making your bedroom a healing haven, a true sanctuary. But there is one other factor which is supremely important. All the space cleansing and feng shui in the world won't help if your bedroom is full of harmful chemicals and gases. It's a horrible thought but your bedroom might actually be making you sick. Any number of health problems can be caused by unseen dangers in our bedrooms—from allergies to headaches, from memory loss to depression.

Our homes are full of hidden hazards. Are your carpets synthetic or foam-backed? They are probably oozing Volatile Organic Compounds (VOCs) such as formaldehyde. Do you have special stain-resistant finishes on your soft furnishings? They most likely leak organo-chlorides and phenols. There are VOCs and organo-chlorines all around the house: in building boards, bedding, paint solvents, adhesives, wood preservatives, household cleaners, air fresheners, polishes, and most plastic products. If your bedroom

lacks adequate ventilation or you rarely open the windows you may have high levels of pollutants building up unchecked.

World-wide it has been estimated that there are around 70,000 synthetic chemicals in use, with another 1,000 added every year. The vast majority are unknown factors: they simply have not been tested fully. We don't know what they do to us and yet we trustingly take them into our homes.

Let's not panic. There are plenty of practical, sensible ways to safeguard yourself in your bedroom.

Choose non-toxic materials

Few of us can afford to redecorate and refurnish our rooms right away. But every time you need to redecorate or choose new furniture make sure you choose safe, non-toxic materials.

- Avoid synthetic foam-backed carpets and instead choose recycled wooden floors; natural floor coverings such as sisal, coir, seagrass, and jute; or 100 percent wool or cotton/wool mix carpets and rugs.
- Look out for paints which are water-based, milk-based, plant, and mineral based. If you want vibrant colors use powdered pigments which you simply mix yourself. Old-fashioned milk paints are long-lasting, safe, and come in a huge range of fashionable and traditional colors. Pick natural thinners such as linseed oil, pine resin turpentine and natural varnishes which allow the wood to breathe (they combine resins with scented turpentine and pigments). The added benefit is that they smell lovely.
- When buying new furniture be careful too. Check what materials are used in the stuffing, base, and fabric of sofas

and chairs. Be very wary of treated materials—they may prevent stains but could be nasty to your health (maybe think about loose covers which can easily be washed instead). Recycled wood is a great option for beds, wardrobes, closets, and chairs. Many companies now use all recycled wood for their furniture and it is not only safer for you but looks great too.

- Pick 100 percent natural fibers for your curtains, covers, and bedlinen. Organic unbleached cotton makes the most wonderful sheets and duvet covers as it gets softer and softer the more you wash it. Snuggling up in them in the winter is pure heaven (but make sure your duvet is all natural too). In the summer, cool linen sheets are about the most inviting fabric you could put on your bed. Be particularly sure your children are sleeping in 100 percent pure materials. Many childhood allergies could be avoided this way. You may put off treating yourself to new bedlinen but I would seriously advise you to change your children's sheets right away. For more advice on healthy, safe rooms for babies and children see the companion book to this, *Spirit of the Nursery.*

- While you're waiting to redecorate or buy new, there are still plenty of things you can do. First of all, keep your bedroom (and your entire home) as well aired and ventilated as possible. Open the windows and let the air in—for at least fifteen minutes twice a day. This also helps to prevent excess humidity and stops the air from getting stale. Maybe install a ceiling fan (they look great and are a must in hot weather).
- Always use natural cleaning products, or make your own with essential oils.
- Make sure everything works in your bedroom. In feng shui terms cracked

window panes, clogged plumbing, and dodgy electrics can negatively affect your health and happiness. Get them fixed as soon as possible. Keep everything running smoothly and efficiently and your life should run along the same way.
- If you live in an area where radon gas is a problem, have your home checked. There are solutions which can remedy the problem.

Safety-proof your bed

It's frightening to think we may be snuggling down in the equivalent of a chemical factory. If your bed is made from chipboard or particleboard (pressed wood shavings held together with resin) it may well be emitting dangerous formaldehyde gases into the air. Formaldehyde has been estimated to cause sensitivity in around a fifth of the

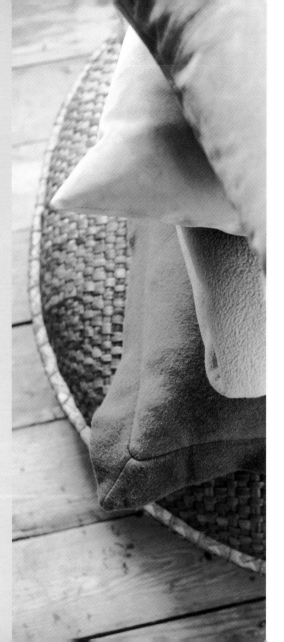

population: symptoms include insomnia, tiredness, coughing, skin rashes, headaches, and throat and eye irritation. It is also a suspected carcinogen (cancer-causing substance). And it's not just the bed either: many bed sheets are coated with a formaldehyde finish that helps prevent wrinkling.

In addition, your mattress and pillows could be stuffed with polyurethane foam which not only makes a pleasant home for allergy-causing dust mites but has also been linked with respiratory problems, and skin and eye irritations. So what do you do?

- Choose iron or untreated solid wood bedframes. Antique (or over ten years old) bedframes are an alternative as most formaldehyde gas will have gone after ten years. However, just to make life even more complicated, iron and steel in bedframes and sprung mattresses can become magnetic and leak EMFs (electro-magnetic fields). Test your bed by running a good compass slowly over a bed—if the needle deflects from north, the springs or mattress are likely to be magnetic.

- Think about switching to a pure cotton mattress—without flame-resistant finishes if at all possible. Futon mattresses are also safe. Choose cotton-filled pillows.
- If you're sensitive to dust mites, buy special mattress and pillow covers. Specialist companies like The Healthy House (www.healthyhouse.co.uk) or American Allergy Supply (www.americanallergy.com) can help.

Banish EMFs

EMFs (electro-magnetic fields) are invisible enemies in your bedroom. They are produced by electricity and emitted by anything that runs on electricity. EMFs have been linked with a range of health problems, from headaches and nausea, to brain tumors and breast cancer. Fortunately it's simple to safeguard your bedroom from their effects.

- If possible keep all electric appliances out of the bedroom, particularly televisions and computers, which give off large amounts. If this isn't possible ensure they are as far away as possible from your bed—the effects of EMFs drop off after about three feet.
- Don't fall asleep with the television on. Unplug all appliances when not in use.
- Swap your electric alarm clock for a battery-powered or old-fashioned wind-up version.
- Electric blankets can expose you to EMFs all through the night. Try warming the bed with hot water bottles. Or, if you really cannot give up your blanket, use it to warm up the bed, then unplug it.

Watch out for geopathic stress

Geopathic stress is caused by abnormal energy fields generated by deep underground streams, large mineral deposits, or faults in the substrata of the earth. It has been suggested that it can be a major contributing factor in everything from migraines to cancer, from nightmares to divorce. The evidence suggests that geopathic stress certainly *does* exist. In Germany it has been researched since the twenties and is taken very seriously. Now builders in Germany and Austria test sites before building and many will routinely give guarantees that new buildings do not have lines of "bad" energy passing through them.

However, even if your bedroom does suffer GS, your health need not necessarily be affected. It comes up through the earth in thin bands or small spirals so will only affect you if you are sleeping directly on top of it all night.

- If you suspect you suffer from GS, try putting cork tiles under your bed for a few weeks and see whether you start to feel better. The tiles seem to neutralize the rays for a limited period. If you do start to feel better, try moving your bed.

- Watch where your pets sleep. Cats adore GS and will often choose to sleep on a bad spot, while dogs will avoid it at all costs. If the cat always makes a bee-line for your bed, try moving it to the dog's favorite spot.

- Babies are apparently very sensitive to GS. If your baby constantly rolls over to one corner of the crib he or she may be trying to escape GS. Move the

crib to another part of the room and see whether the baby stays put.
- If you feel you are affected by GS try the following: switch on a hairdryer and run it all over you with the side of the dryer touching your body. It sounds crazy but try it once a week—it does appear to help.

Planning your Bedroom

Now it's time to look back at your treasure map. Have any themes appeared? If not, try these exercises. Jot down your first impressions, however silly (they may be illuminating).

1 Which five words would you use to describe your ideal bedroom?

2 Think back to bedrooms you have slept in in the past. Which were the most appealing?

3 Are there any movies or books which have bedrooms which trigger your imagination? What are their elements?

4 Write down five smells you would like in your bedroom.

5 Write down five sounds you would like to hear in your bedroom.

6 Write down five sensations you would like to feel in your bedroom.

7 Write down five things you would like to do in your bedroom.

8 Can you paint your perfect bedroom? It might just be colors or shapes rather than a literal representation.

9 If you could have a "fantasy" bedroom, without thought of budget or practicality, what would it be like?

Your answers should allow you to build up some idea of what you might like in your bedroom. In actual fact, most fantasies can be achieved—or at least a good approximation of them. As anyone who has watched the numerous house "makeovers" on television knows, you can do an awful lot (sometimes too much!) with a small budget and a large imagination. In case you're still having trouble coming up with ideas, let's think about some possibilities.

Generally speaking, bedrooms fall into three distinct categories. These are outlined below in very broad, crude strokes. You may want your own bedroom to incorporate elements from several different types.

Serene slumber palace

This is a place where sleep is taken very seriously. Other activities may take place here but above all else it is a temple of dreams. These rooms should be kept as simple as possible—so nothing intrudes on your consciousness. Obviously the bed is of extreme importance—it could be of any design but above all is built for extreme comfort. Invest in the best quality mattress you can afford and, in my experience, the largest size bed you can accommodate. Bed coverings are vitally important too, so go for supreme comfort.

Inspiration could come from:
- Log cabins—warm and cocooning, tucked away from the outside world, simple rustic wood with the heavenly scent of pine. Think of homespun fabrics and woollen rugs, knitted cushions, tartan curtains.
- Country cottages—cosy and welcoming, simple and childlike. Flower-sprigged cottons or stripes and checks, old lace, eiderdowns, and jugs of wild flowers.
- The night sky—stars, planets, the moon. Dark, embracing indigos and midnight blues; glimmering stars on the ceiling; and plenty of candles.
- Dreams and visions—soft, ethereal colors, evoking dreams. Murals of delicate dream or fantasy images. Furniture evoking castles, or palaces.
- Japanese simplicity—clean lines and low-level living. Tatami matting, futons, bamboo screens, paper lanterns, sculptural flowers, origami mobiles.
- Temples and sanctuaries—cool, calm, and serene. Trompe l'oeil columns, statues of goddesses, a large bowl with water and floating petals.

Raunchy boudoir

Yes, O.K, you sleep in here (a bit) but by far the most important role of this bedroom is sex. You'll have a robust bed but also consider other furniture which might have interesting possibilities— squashy bean bags or floor cushions for instance. Texture is wildly important—all the old clichés of satin sheets (yes, they do feel gorgeous) and fur rugs work well but also titillate your senses with velvet, fleece, rubber, and feathers. Lighting should be versatile—to suit your changing moods. Although having mirrors in your bedroom is not great feng shui, this kind of bedroom won't be able to resist at least one.

Inspiration could come from:

- Bohemian-style brothel—clashing fabrics and textures such as velvet and embroidered silk, stained glass lanterns, screens, and gilded mirrors.

- Arabian tent—an exotic desert hideaway with fabric covering the walls and looping up to the center of the ceiling. Kilims on the floor, low tables with copper bowls of nibbles and goblets for wine.
- Pacific holiday—Hawaiian garlands, fresh fruit, sea, and sand. Kitsch and wild, think about plastic palm trees, bamboo beach mats, sounds of the ocean.
- Jungle fever—lush vegetation, tropical colors, exotic animals. Go wild in the jungle with ropes slung across the room, animal prints, fake fur rugs, rush matting, jungle sounds.
- Hollywood boudoir—all satin and silk, faded pastels, Art Deco lights, favorite movie posters or photographs, lingerie and lounge suits, dramatic dressing gowns, candelabra, and (of course) a casting couch.

Sacred space

This bedroom is a "time out" zone, a place of private meditation and ritual, or simply somewhere to hide away and read and think. This bedroom may well have a desk or escritoire, possibly a bookcase or shelf for favorite tomes, a comfortable armchair or (if space allows) a small sofa or daybed. It's a place to fire the imagination and soothe the soul so it will have plenty of interesting objects and pictures. The bed will be a cosy retreat—snuggling up with a good book is as important as sleeping or lovemaking here. This kind of room runs the risk of becoming cluttered more easily than the other two so make sure you have plenty of good, attractive storage. If your waking activities start to ruin your sleep it may be an idea to invest in a nice screen which can be placed in front of your desk or books.

Inspiration for this kind of room could come from:

- Writers' retreats or artists' studios—a neat, measured Jane Austen-style room or a wild Bloomsbury Group haven. An easel to display your favorite inspirational pictures and art materials for when the mood strikes.
- Teepees and yurts, ethnic weavings, earthy pots, colorful patterns; musical instruments; a CD player for drumming or guided visualizations.
- Woodland glades, wood and stone, running water, and nature spirits. A woodland painted on your walls, jugs of wild flowers, herbs, and branches. Willow figures and woven baskets.
- Seaside huts and cottages—fresh blues and white, driftwood, shells, cotton ticking, deck flooring. Models of boats and seabirds.

Darkness and light

Of all the rooms in the house, the bedroom is the one in which it is most important to get the balance between darkness and light just right. Curiously, it's something about which we don't often think. Yet light and dark affect us just as much as color, sound, and scent. Now we have electric lights we are no longer governed by the daily cycle of sun and moon so much, yet part of us still remembers the days when we would rise with the sun and go to bed with the sunset. According to the ancient Indian system of ayurveda, that is still the healthiest way to live our daily lives. I'm not suggesting you get up with the lark every morning (although everyone should see a sunrise once in a while) but it can be quite illuminating to become aware of how we are subtly affected by the light in our homes.

Natural light changes throughout the day and in each and every season. It never stays the same. Even moonlight changes throughout the moon's monthly cycle. Yet we tend to bathe our rooms in solid blocks of artificial light. Try to introduce various kinds of lighting so you can alter the mood as and when you want. Try these tips for introducing the full spectrum of light into your bedroom:

- Keep your curtains open at night and enjoy the phases of the moon. Some people find that moonlight can give them very vivid dreams but do try a spot of moon-bathing occasionally.
- Change your bulbs to natural day-light bulbs wherever possible. They are more expensive but well worth the outlay.
- Keep lighting flexible. Do you sit under the overhead watchful eye of just one

central light? Add more light sources so you can alter the mood of your bedroom. You need a good bright light by your bed for reading but you could also have uplighters, floor and wall lamps to help create mood and atmosphere. Install dimmer switches to give you even more flexibility.

- Be inventive. Almost anything can be transformed into a lamp nowadays—investigate lights made of rock salt (they give off beneficial negative ions), lava lamps, oil lamps. Some lights project moving scenes onto your walls; others can project a whole scene onto a wall. If you're creative you can make your own light shades (molding fabric over ready-made frames) or painting scenes on large paper shades to fix over light bulbs (check the safety).

- Shadow and shade is just as important as light, particularly if you live in a hot, sunny climate. Wooden slatted shutters create a cool haven of shade from the heat of the sun. Soft billowy muslin and gauze diffuse the light into softness—you can cool the effect even more by choosing limpid shades of blue and green. Canopies and awnings over windows can reduce the glare, while growing plants and creepers around the house and windows can deflect the heat.

- If you live in a city and never see the dark, think about investing in a pair of heavy drapes or solid wooden shutters for your bedroom. You may find you sleep much better—although make sure fresh air can still circulate through your room.

The Bedroom of the Senses

A good bedroom should delight all the senses. It needs to be a space which is truly inviting, alluring, and enticing: a place which thrills the eye, gladdens the ear, and delights the nose; a place full of things which beg to be touched and stroked. We're entering the world of Aphrodite, the goddess not just of love, but of beauty.

Color in the bedroom

Color has the power to lift our spirits, to soothe our souls, to enliven us, or calm us—it is the supreme mood shifter. The wonderful thing about color is that it offers one of the quickest, easiest, and most satisfying ways of completely changing the mood of your bedroom. Slapping on a fresh coat of paint is quick and inexpensive, and if you don't like the effect you've created you can simply paint it out and start afresh. Play with color, have fun with it, experiment. There are no rules other than those you impose on yourself. Sometimes the best results come about through happy accidents.

As a general rule, bedrooms are usually furnished in the cooler colors, those with shorter wavelengths (blue, green, and violet tones). But it's really totally up to you. Below are the attributes generally ascribed to each color.

RED: Red is the color of fire; it can be oppressive and tiring if you stay in an intensely red room for too long. It's not a great color to choose for bedrooms and studies, except in accent colors or very soft pale rose tones. You can, however, use red tones to lift a bedroom which feels cold—add a rich warm paisley throw, luscious cushions, crimson lamp-shades, or a vibrant rug or kilim.

PINK: Pink is soft, nurturing, and pretty—very traditional in its softer incarnations for country-style bedrooms. Be bolder and it can become a quite different beast; shocking pink or fuchsia are vibrant and slightly wild. It may be a bit much for all-over color but one wall might look stunning. If you really want to make a bold statement, go for the shocking pink of silks and saris—it's a great color for a bedspread, blind, or a few glamorous cushions or pillows.

ORANGE: Orange is the color of confidence, of joy, and sociability. Again, it's not often the first choice for bedrooms. However, there are a great variety of tones and some could work in bedrooms. Think of Etruscan vases and Italian frescoes; dusty, dusky yellowy oranges can look wonderful.

YELLOW: Yellow lifts the spirits, banishes depression, and raises your energy levels. It will cheer up almost any room, particularly if you team it with soft creamy colors (and remember that blue looks great with yellow too). Yellow, particuarly the brighter shades, can be a bit too energetic for bedrooms but can be useful for cold, north-facing rooms as it's wonderful to wake up with.

GREEN: Our eye muscles don't need to adjust to green so it is a color which can bring harmony, contentment, and calm. It's not commonly used in bedrooms but can work well. It's a particularly good choice if your bedroom needs to double up as a sitting room or work-room.

BLUE: Blue is supremely restful and soothing. It calms the central nervous system and can lower stress. Blue is a perfect color for bedrooms but may need warming up with other colors as it can be a little cool. Yellow and warm browns work well with blue.

INDIGO: Shades of indigo are said to enhance psychic powers and to promote day-dreaming. Soft indigo shades could be perfect for a peaceful bedroom. A shot of sheer indigo can make a striking accent color.

VIOLET: Violet calms the spirit at the deepest level. It also soothes both body and mind. Therapists use violet for insomnia and tension so it can be a very useful color for bedrooms. Think about soft lilac, lavender, and foxglove shades; the soft blue-violet of hyacinth. All these can be delightful in bedrooms and will give a sense of peace and tranquility.

WHITE: White can be very stark. However, if you break it up with the odd burst of color it can be soothing and effective. There are many shades of white now available and if you use toning shades of white: egg white, bone white, or milk white—or the softer creamier tones of oatmeal, calico, straw, and wax white—you can create a simple yet sophisticated effect.

BROWN: Much despised over recent years as a decorating color, brown is making a come-back—yes, even in the bedroom. The darker browns can be a bit gloomy as an overall shade (with the exception of wooden paneling) but they look wonderful as accent colors.

Other thoughts on color

- Introduce colored glass into your bedroom. It doesn't need to be a whole window, it could be just a panel. Alternatively, hang a piece of stained glass in a window to catch the light.
- Let rainbows dance around your bedroom by hanging a few multi-faceted crystals in windows where they will catch the sunshine.
- If you fancy a simple change of style for next to nothing, buy a roll of inexpensive muslin or calico and dye it yourself. Fabric dyes are surprisingly easy to use and cheap to buy and they come in a huge array of sumptuous colors. Use the fabric to make curtains, to cover furniture, to create "secret" areas by hanging lengths from the ceiling, or to create an exotic Arabian Nights bed (billowing folds of several shades of the desert).

- Painting junk furniture can also be great fun, and brings a splash of color into any room. Can't paint? Try decoupage—you can achieve amazing effects for little outlay.
- Experiment with colored light bulbs and colored cellophane over the light fitting. Red lights could also bring some added spice to the bedroom!
- Change the mood of your bedroom according to the season. In the past it was common to have "summer" and "winter" curtains. If you choose cheaper fabrics you could have as many as suit your mood.

The scented bedroom

The ancient Greeks believed that beautiful scents were a means of contacting the gods. They possessed an

Essential oils in the bedroom

Before we start, let's just cover a few ground rules. First, oils should be pure. True oils will vary greatly in price depending on the oil you choose, so if all the oils are the same price or if you're offered rose or neroli oil very cheaply then you can be sure it's not the real thing. Second, essential oils should always be used with respect. Never use more than the stated amounts, never take them internally, and never put them straight on your skin without the advice of a qualified aromatherapist. Some oils should not be used during pregnancy or by those with health problems—if you have any doubts, consult a professional.

There are loads of ways to use oils—in oil burners and diffusers (or there are special rings which are put directly on light bulbs), or just add a few drops of oil to a bowl of hot water.

entire language of perfumery in which flowery scents were chosen to invoke peace, joy, or even pure sensuality. So, if you want to turn your bedroom into a delicious haven for the senses, indulge your nostrils. Scent is a powerful but also infinitely subtle way of shifting the atmosphere in a room.

Let's not even think about those horrible synthetic room fragrances and air fresheners—please. Instead turn to natural fragrances: flowers, herbs, and, above all, aromatherapy.

Which oils do you choose?

Really the choice is totally up to you and your nose, but certain oils do have the ability to impart a particular mood to your bedroom.

RELAXING OILS: These are the soothers and pacifiers—oils to use when you want to stop the world and float away. Try camomile, clary sage, frankincense, jasmine, lavender, marjoram, melissa, neroli, rose.

CALMING, REASSURING OILS: These are great when you're feeling anxious or apprehensive. Fill your bedroom with reassuring scents such as geranium, jasmine, lavender, melissa, neroli, palmarosa, and ylang ylang.

UPLIFTING OILS: For times when you're feeling down and depressed or swamped by negativity, bergamot (a serious friend in need), camomile, hyssop, lavender, orange, or yarrow are invaluable.

SENSUALITY OILS: Ideal for the great seduction scene. Go for a heady brew chosen from jasmine, rose, sandalwood, tuberose, ylang ylang.

SERENITY OILS: Perfect for meditation or for when you need to switch off and turn inwards. Try camomile, francincense, juniper, linden blossom, rose, sandalwood, vetiver.

SICKROOM OILS: Keep the bugs away with a brew of some of these oils—eucalyptus, pine, rosemary, tea tree. Add some lavender to soothe the invalid.

Further tips

Once you start getting into the sense of smell, it can be hard to stop. Here are a few other ideas to fragrance the bedroom.

- Flowers are the most subtle and absolutely the most beautiful way to introduce scent into your bedroom. Fill your room with the aroma of carnations, freesias, gardenias, hyacinths, jasmine, lilac, lilies, lily of the valley, mimosa, narcissi, primroses, roses (of course), scented geraniums, stocks, sweet peas, tuberose, and violets.
- Display sweet-smelling plants close to your windows so the scent wafts through: lilac, jasmine, honeysuckle, roses, night-scented stocks, wallflowers, lavender, mignonette, mock orange, heliotrope, and so on.
- Make your own scented drawer liners. Spray simple lining paper with a plant mister containing a few drops of your

chosen oil and pure spring water. Try cedarwood, lavender, geranium, vetiver, or lemon. Put them scented-side down in the drawers and fill with clothes. Top up the scent by spraying the paper every few months.
- Pretty lavender bags (made from old-fashioned lace, crisp gingham, or vivid silk) give a sweet, fresh scent to your clothes and linens. Make sure you store clean bedding with lavender bags.
- Add 3–5 drops of oil to the softener compartment of the washing machine to scent bedlinen. You can tumble clothes with scent by putting two drops of oil onto a handkerchief-sized piece of fabric and adding it to the load: lavender, rosemary, geranium, rosewood, jasmine, and ylang-ylang all work well.
- Invest in loads of scented candles (but choose real aromatherapy ones).

The "Feel-Good" Bedroom

A bedroom should invigorate and entice all the senses. It should be more than a "look-good" space, more even than a "smell-good" place. It needs to be a "feel-good" room. By choosing furniture, fabrics, and furnishings in a wide variety of textures you can do far more than make your bedroom just look interesting and attractive. Every time your hands, feet, or face (or indeed any part of you) come into contact with a different texture, it makes you focus on your body; it pulls you back out of your mind into a real sense of the here and now. Let's start by thinking about the various components of the bedroom and the choices you have for each.

Floors

Floors matter deeply in a bedroom. Second to the bathroom, this is the room in which you are most likely to go barefoot—or just plain bare. So it needs to feel good (and smell good), as well as look good. It's not just your feet either: wood is supportive if you're planning on yoga sessions in your bedroom, while a

really good fake fur rug feels wantonly sensuous for languid lovemaking.

Think about what you want to greet your toes as you get out of bed in the morning, or in the middle of the night when perhaps the heating is not on. Stone is not a great choice—unless you live in a really hot climate and crave coolness. Anyone else would need to warm it up with rugs. Wood can work well, but ensure it's unsplintered. Again, rugs might be needed for cooler climes. Natural mattings, wonderful though they are, are not usually at their best in the bedroom to my mind. They are a bit too hairy for rolling on (with the exception of seagrass) and just don't have the comfort factor I feel a bedroom needs.

Boring though it may sound, carpet is often the best bet. It's warm and kind to feet and bodies. As bedrooms don't tend to have heavy traffic passing through, your choice should be much wider than

in other, more public, rooms such as living rooms. Think bold. If you've always hankered after foot-deep shagpile, this is your opportunity.

Walls

Paper or paint? They're the obvious choices, but there are others. We often forget walls can feel nice as well as look good but just think about the rough uneven surface of old plaster, the molded contours of wood paneling, the sheer slide of glass, the cool density of stone. Don't just stick to paint and plain paper; be a little imaginative. In the olden days it was common to "paper" walls with fabrics. Nowadays it only tends to be the very rich who can afford such luxuries but, as bedrooms are often small, you could try "fabric-ing" yours—or choose very cheap fabric and dye, or decorate it to your own design. Tapestries were a

variation on the theme but again, genuine tapestries are very expensive. However, you could buy a large piece of beautiful fabric and give it the tapestry treatment by hanging it on a large wooden or gilded pole.

Fabrics

Feel the difference between silk and mohair, velvet and cashmere, linen and corduroy. Check out how pure wool feels next to a synthetic fiber; how a pure cotton varies from one mixed with acrylic. Don't just feel them with your fingers; run the fabric over your face, against your cheek.

Cottons and linens are wonderful fabrics if you want your room to feel brisk and bright, or cool and calm. They are businesslike, honest, and friendly. They feel cool to the skin and so make wonderful bedlinens—there is nothing more divine than sliding between pure linen or 100 percent fine cotton sheets on a hot, clammy summer's evening. On the other hand, if you wanted to bring a warm, cocooning, cozy feel to a bedroom you might investigate fabrics which are softer, more gentle, and enveloping. Soft 100 percent wool gives a welcoming warmth; so does chenille and brushed cotton. Moleskin and peached fabrics make you want to snuggle up. Add a few veritable "comfort blankets" made in mohair or alpaca and you won't want to leave the nest.

However, if you want to usher in a mood of pure sensuality there are some highly seductive fabrics willing to play romantic games. Velvet is the prime seducer—soft, voluptuous, and totally abandoned. Plain, crushed, devoré: play with all three. It can be a delicate fabric so

it's not such a great idea for furnishing, though you can get away with the same effect by using a heavier velour—Aphrodite would still approve. Silk and satin have become synonymous with sexy bedclothes and it's true that there is little to beat the feel of satin against bare skin. However, satin sheets are a bit hackneyed (and a devil to wash) so maybe introduce satin in other guises: on pillows and cushions, bed covers, or drapes for a four-poster? Fur, of course, is the other prime sensation-provider, beloved of medieval bedchambers, but as no-one with a conscience can bear to buy fur we'll have to give that one a miss unless you have an ancient fur stuffed in a closet or find a thrift store bargain. Some designers are now playing with quite realistic fake furs which make superb pillows and throws—check out the fashion fabric departments.

Trimmings

If you can't afford to buy new furniture or put up new drapes or soft furnishings, then go wild with some new trimmings. The finishing touches you add can totally change the appearance—and feel—of a room. Plain cotton curtains could be invested with a deep fringe or an added border in a more tactile fabric. Tie-backs and tassels can transform curtains—they come in all kinds of fabrics, from chenille to silk, from wool to gold thread. Or you could make your own. Ribbons, fringing, and ropes can give new life to an old blind or bedspread. Beads give good feel-nice sensations too. You could make a fringe of them to edge a bedroom curtain or go totally wild and make a new curtain entirely out of beads (experiment with glass, ceramic, and wooden beads to see which feels nicest as you push through its tendrils).

Other thoughts on texture

- Don't restrict yourself to the furnishing fabric department; look at dress fabrics too—they can make wonderful pillows, cushions, and throws.
- If you knit, make yourself some seriously desirable throws, blankets, and pillows in a variety of wools—from cool cottons to luxurious mohair and alpaca. Cable-knits in earthy homespun or creamy Aran give texture and coziness combined and are far too good to keep just for clothes.
- Use pebbles and shells as interesting door knobs. Feel the difference between something smooth and round and something rough and gritty. Put different knobs on each drawer for a totally sense-expanding experience.
- Think about using fabrics in unusual ways. Why should toweling just be for towels, or quilts just for beds? A thick quilt could cover a drafty door, and would look and feel wonderful. Where is it written in stone that a tablecloth should always stay a tablecloth when it could make fabulous curtains?

Furniture

We've talked about beds briefly but let's think a little more about this most vital piece of furniture. It's one place where your imagination should really run wild. If you already have a very serviceable bed, you don't need to change it, you can just give it a facelift. How about adding on an interesting headboard or footboard? Lift or lower the legs (or change them entirely). If you find a local woodworker he or she would be able to accommodate most fantasies, be it a fairy-tale four-poster, lit bateau, a chunky oversized

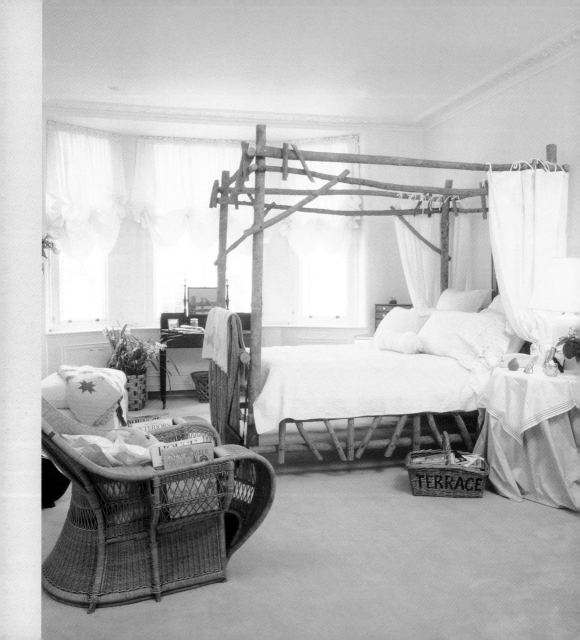

Three Bears-type bed, or a clean no-nonsense minimal look.

Of course it doesn't need to be straightforward wood (though frankly I don't ever think wood is exactly "straightforward"). You might think about other natural materials like willow, bamboo, or fabric (go wild with your choice of fabric for headboards—you don't have to have the typical buttoned upholstered look, straight runs of fabric looks fabulous).

Bedside tables are usually a must—a place for the bedside book, diary, or dream journal, a glass of water, a bedroom crystal. Make sure they are the right height so you can reach the items on them comfortably and you're not likely to hit yourself on them during the night. If you fancy something different, think about a cube of pure wood; or an old chest (useful storage too), a bench, a painted filing cabinet.

You need storage for clothes (unless you're lucky enough to have your own dressing room). Long runs of fitted cupboards are practical but look a bit dated (if you can't change them, maybe fit a beautiful curtain rail above and cover them with some interesting fabric). Alternatively, customize with paint effects. Free-standing furniture is more flexible. Try to keep it at a minimum though, or your room will become over-burdened with furniture. Think about alternatives to standard bedroom furniture too: a stack of interesting cases or boxes, map chests (if you have the space), huge wicker baskets. Who says it has to be "bedroom" furniture? Think about bringing in a sideboard (for a curious sixties look) or a desk instead of a dressing table. Kitchen storecupboards could be customized to become alternative wardrobes. A coffee table can work well in a large bedroom—with beanbags or low seating around it.

The Natural Bedroom

Bringing nature into your bedroom means surrounding yourself with the healing and blessing of the outside world. It puts us in touch, in the tiniest of ways, with Mother Earth and Father Sky, with the old sacred pull of the planet. It also welcomes in all the old gods and goddesses, spirits and angels of the wild and forgotten places.

Wood

Let's start to bring the natural world into the bedroom by looking at wood. Wood is a living, breathing entity with myriad colors, scents, and textures. Most tribal peoples believe that each tree has its own soul. The Maori of New Zealand are said to despair as each tree is cut down as the souls will have nowhere to go on earth and so will return to the stars— leaving us poorer for their loss. The Celts honored trees as having spirits and being great friends or dangerous foes. There are heroic tales of the souls of trees going into battle for their human friends and often dying because they stayed away from their tree too long.

When wood is young and green it exudes energy and enthusiasm. As it gets older and more seasoned, it is imbued with wisdom and a warm, protective energy. Wood is embracing, nurturing, loving, and healing. Use it where you can but be sure not to plunder the forests in doing so. Always use recycled wood if you can or, if it must be new, make absolutely sure it comes from sustainable, environmentally sensitive sources. Shun like the plague endangered tropical hardwoods such as teak, mahogany, and lauan. If you are decorating, consider leaving natural woods bare, or gently polish them with linseed oil to bring out the subtle beauty of their grains.

A wooden bed is a joy to sleep in. Consider commissioning one from a local craftsman, using naturally harvested or reclaimed timber. It can echo any style you wish: from serene modern lines to traditional carved and decorated. Sleigh beds, four posters, low-slung, simple, ornate, wildly over-the-top—it's up to you. Think too about shifting proportions—how about a bed which is over-sized and high off the floor? Or a bed with the usual legs removed and thick stumpy rough-hewn ones added instead.

Stone

Stone is earthing, grounding, and strengthening. If you feel a bit divorced from reality or if you have a relationship which is rocky, bring the earth element into your bedroom. Stone can be chilly underfoot but could be used for window ledges or introduced in bowls, statues, or just simply display beautiful stones from nature.

There are certain stones you just have to pick up and touch. Whether you find them lying on the bed of a fast-moving stream, in a rock pool, or simply huddled among the millions on a pebble-clad beach, there is always one which somehow finds its way into your pocket. Most magical of all are the so-called "witch" stones, pebbles with natural holes in them which are supposedly protective and magical. Use them all over your house.

Crystals

There is a whole healing art devoted to the use of crystals but I love them for the look and feel of them, regardless of what they are doing to me. The great healer Denise Linn suggests choosing one particular crystal as your bedroom crystal. Cleanse it by mixing together a solution of one cup of spring water and half a cup of salt. Bury your crystal in the mixture and allow to soak for at least 24 hours. Then you can dedicate your crystal to the energy you would like in your room. Simply hold it and focus your energy and intention into it. Then keep it safe somewhere in your room.

There are so many kinds of crystals they are too numerous to mention. The following should get you started...

- **Amethyst**: Calming, soothing, and cleansing; it will help you meditate and give you a good night's sleep.
- **Jade**: Increases vitality; healing and harmonizing; protective. This beautiful crystal is said to help prolong life and put things in perspective.
- **Lapis Lazuli**: A very spiritual stone, said to protect against evil spirits. It also

guards against depression, helps you express yourself creatively and artistically, boosts mental clarity, and promotes spiritual awakening. Keep one by your bed.

- **Moonstone**: A stone to calm turbulent emotions, to heighten intuition, and open up the subconscious. A very feminine stone, it can bring a gentle yin quality to over-masculine rooms. Keep in a bedroom for useful dreams.

- **Rose Quartz**: A beautiful symbol of love, beauty, the family, children, and creativity. Also promotes peace and self-esteem. It is lovely for babies and children's rooms in particular but all bedrooms generally.

Fire

Fire brings energy into a room. It is also very protecting. A lighted candle by your bed will soothe your spirits. A night-light in a child's bedroom will keep all those scary monsters at bay. However, always remember that fire can be dangerous. Never leave a fire or candle unattended. If you are using night-lights or long-lasting candles, make sure they are secure in their holder and put the holder in a bowl of water or sand large enough so that the candle would be extinguished by the water or sand should it fall over.

Candles are the most common way we bring the element of fire into our homes. The color of candle you choose might simply match or provide a contrast for your decorating scheme or it could signify an inner purpose. If you like the idea of some candle magic try using these colors:

- **PINK**: When you're seeking love or wanting to conceive a child.
- **GREEN**: When someone is ill; the color green brings balance, harmony, peace, hope, growth, and healing. It is also thought to increase abundance and wealth.
- **YELLOW**: For joy and friendship; to increase concentration, wisdom, communication, and good luck.
- **RED**: When you want some extra passion, energy, vibrant life, and love in your life.
- **ORANGE**: For joy and happiness.
- **BLUE**: When you're meditating or feeling frazzled and tense.
- **PURPLE**: When you're seeking deeper dreams or spiritual awareness.
- **WHITE**: Whenever! This general-purpose candle can be used at any time.

Concentrate on your purpose before and while you light the candle. You could also use it for meditation to strengthen your desire.

Water

Water soothes and calms the soul; it is purifying and healing.

- To bring the energy of water into your room, and particularly if your house is lacking humidity, have bowls of clean, fresh water around. You could transform them into ornaments in their own right by choosing attractive bowls and adding beautiful pebbles, shells, and rocks to the bottom or alternatively, try floating petals or whole flower heads on top.
- Spray your room regularly with a mister. Space clearers say that misting

can neutralize unpleasant emotional charges left in a room and can add in healing negative ions. Use spring water —you can also add homeopathic remedies or flower essences for extra emotional impact. Alternatively, choose the ready-made flower remedy sprays already mentioned.

- Leave a bowl of water out on a moonlit night to "catch" the moonlight. Put the bowl next to your bed to promote interesting dreams.

Air

Air is all around us but it can easily become stagnant and heavy in a house. Think of the fresh invigorating air of a mountain, a forest, or a seaside cliff-top. Now follow these steps to bring the full power of the element of air into your bedroom.

- Rooms need to breathe, so open windows and ensure a cross-flow of air through your home.
- Improve the quality of your air (particularly if you live in the city or next to a busy road) by using an ionizer to make your air smell fresher and feel more energizing.
- Fans keep the air moving, keep you cool, and can look stylish too; choose old-fashioned ceiling fans or funky chrome floor fans.
- Incense, smudging, and burning aromatherapy oils are all recommended by ancient cultures for attracting the spirits of the air. However, you need to go easy in bedrooms with the first two as the scents can be a bit too pungent for everyday use. If you do smudge or burn incense, I'd advise you do it well in advance of bedtime.

Blessing and Rituals

By now your bedroom should be shaping up nicely. You should have a clear, calming flow of energy and have furnished and decorated it to suit your heart and soul. In this final chapter, let's look at some practices which you can use to ensure your bedroom remains the perfect sanctuary.

Bedroom blessings

Rituals are important. Ceremonies, however small and seemingly insignificant, bring a sense of purpose and peace to everyday life. They offer a chance to be still for a while, to take stock, to balance yourself amid the hurly-burly of normal days.

These rituals are all very simple yet highly effective. Try them out and see how they feel. But do bear in mind that they are only suggestions—you don't have to follow them to the letter. Feel free to shift elements, or add your own words, actions, or props. They need to be "your" rituals.

Consecrating your bedroom

This lovely blessing calls on your guardian angel to consecrate your bedroom. You will need a candle, an oil burner (or a bowl of hot water), some lavender essential oil, and four pebbles or small crystals.

1 Sit in the center of the room and breathe quietly and calmly—don't concentrate on the breath or force it, just allow it to deepen naturally.

2 Reach out with your awareness and try to get a sense of the room around you. What atmosphere does it have? What atmosphere do you want it to have?

3 Light a candle and ask your own guardian angel to come near and bring love and peace to your bedroom. You might have a sense of a divine, loving being embracing you with its soft wings. (Note: if you have experience of other guardians, such as power animals or deities from various religions, you can equally call upon them here).

4 Let five drops of lavender oil fall into the water of your burner or bowl. As each drop hits the water imagine a spark of loving energy (like a tiny fairy) flying out from the oil to each corner of the room. The last drop's energy shoots to the center of the room. Imagine your angel smiling with pleasure at the lavender spirits.

5 Ask the gentle spirits of the lavender to bring you peace, rest, relaxation, and sweet dreams.

6 Imagine your aura (an egg-shaped bubble of energy around your body) becoming suffused with a beautiful soft

pinkish-gold color. Allow that soft colored light to expand beyond your aura, growing until it embraces the entire room.

7 Hold the pebbles or crystals in your hand and imagine them, too, imbued with the pink-gold light. Place one pebble in each corner of the room to hold the love and light intact throughout your space.

8 Thank your guardian angel—you may also ask for any particular blessing or protection. In return, envisage a flame of pure love shooting from your heart to your angel.

9 Softly blow out the candle and the oil burner, if you are using one. If you have chosen a bowl of hot water you can leave that in place.

Bedtime cleansing ritual

This gentle blessing marks the break from day to night and eases you into sweet dreams.

1 Run a deep bath, then mix a few drops of your favorite aromatherapy oil (lavender, camomile, or geranium work well for this ritual) in a little milk and add to the water.

2 As you undress, visualize all your daytime anxieties dropping away. As you take off any make-up and brush your teeth, imagine all the negativity of the day being cleansed away.

3 Soak in the bath, allowing any vestiges of irritation and worry to be washed away. Gently pat yourself dry and put on your night clothes.

4 Light an oil burner by your bed and add four drops of lavender oil. If you prefer you can put the oils on a tissue and keep them by your pillow. If you have a bedroom crystal, place it by your bed to protect you through the night.

5 Lie down and, as you breathe in the soothing scent of the oil, cast your mind back over the day. Review it without judgment. Start at the beginning of the day and end as you are now, in bed.

6 If you are feeling tense or stressed, run through your body, in turn tensing every muscle in your body and then releasing it. Screw up your toes, tense your calves, pull back your knees; tense your thighs and buttocks. Pull in your stomach, your abdomen, tighten your chest. Make fists, tense your arms, shrug your shoulders. Screw up your face and take a deep breathe in, hold, and let it all go. Repeat again.

7 Is anything still worrying you? Scribble down any worrying thoughts on a pad by your bed. You can deal with them in the morning.

8 Now ask your guardian angel or other guardian to watch over your bed and send you sweet or useful dreams. If you have a power animal you could ask it to accompany you on a healing or useful journey in your sleep.

9 Blow out your burner and feel the soft, sweet breath of your angel or animal brush gently against your cheek as you drop into a deep peaceful sleep.

There are plenty of other rituals you could perform in your bedroom. You might think about:

• Waking up and greeting the day rituals. Try some yoga (the Salutation to the Sun is ideal) or some tai chi.

• Sacred sex rituals. Tantric and taoist practices offer some wonderful sensual and sexual rituals. Explore these incredible traditions.

- Releasing negativity. Don't allow your frustrations and annoyances to fester. Maybe use some aura cleansing or visualization. Or put your gripes literally on ice (write them down, put them into a container of water, and freeze). It helps, honestly.

Bedroom altar

We humans have always built altars or shrines, it seems. Evidence from neolithic times shows our ancient ancestors kept certain places sacred and invested them with a numinous quality. But nowadays few Western homes (apart from those belonging to people with an orthodox faith) have any vestige of sacred places or shrines. Yet an altar is a simple thing to erect. All it takes is a small space—it could be a window ledge, a

table top, part of a dressing table, a bookshelf... I'm quite willing to bet that maybe, in a small or totally unconscious way, you have already made some kind of altar in your bedroom. Maybe it's a couple of beloved photographs; perhaps a crystal or a candle. You might have an incense burner and have positioned a vase of flowers next to it.

These are altars in themselves—small places of focus which make you want to stop, pause, ponder, say a prayer maybe, or remember someone with love. What you put on your altar is totally up to you. But they should be things that speak directly to your soul. Not "look-good" things, not even particularly "feel-good" things, but things that have a deep resonance for you. Sometimes the items on an altar can be very soothing but more often they will trigger all manner of emotions: tapping into your soul lessons. They might even make you recall

and ponder your fears, your insecurities, your needs.

If you are not sure what to put on your altar, then follow the old tried and tested formulae. In most traditional cultures, an altar is built using things that represent the four elements. So earth is honored with something living, such as a plant, or with the fabric of the earth—a stone, a bowl of earth, maybe a ceramic pot, or a beautiful piece of wood. Air is traditionally represented by incense as the smoke moves through the air towards heaven—you can easily buy incense sticks or freshly made incense which you burn using a charcoal block on a fire-proof container. If you're not keen on incense you could substitute an aromatherapy oil burner with the same effect. Fire is obviously represented by candles. Water can easily be evoked with a bowl of clear fresh water

or something brought from the ocean or river—some sand, a pebble, or shell. In addition, you could add a favorite image—maybe a mandala, a goddess, saint, or angel; perhaps a statue; a crystal, some beautiful fresh flowers...

Time for bed...

So there it is, the end of this little book and time to say "good night." I hope it's helped you discover your ideal bedroom and given you some ideas beyond fancy paint effects and various bizarre ways to use MDF! Above all, I'd like to think it's helped you turn your bedroom, however small or apparently insignificant, into a truly healing space, a sanctuary for body, mind, and soul. I wish you good nights, bright and cheery mornings, and sweet dreams.

Resources

Space clearing sprays

Pacific Essences **www.pacificessences.com**
For a good source of essences try the International
Flower Essence Repertoire **flower@atlas.co.uk**

Further reading

- *Spirit of the Home* by Jane Alexander (Watson-
  Guptill). The mythology, psychology, and energetics
  of the home.
- *Sacred Rituals at Home* by Jane Alexander. More ideas
  for blessings and rituals.
- *In a Spiritual Style* by Laura Cerwinske. Great
  inspiration for using religious icons.
- *Interior Design with Feng Shui* by Sarah Rossbach. To
  my mind, still the best introduction to feng shui.
- *Creating Sacred Space with Feng Shui* by Karen
  Kingston. A great guide to space clearing.
- *Space Clearing* by Denise Linn. Another great space
  clearing book.

- *The New Natural House Book* by David Pearson.
  Good if you want to go deeper into the idea
  of eco-home.
- *The Fragrant Pharmacy* by Valerie Ann Worwood. A
  truly practical introduction to using essential oils.
- *The Illustrated Guide to Crystals* by Judy Hall.
  Gives more information on crystals and their
  healing influence.
- *The Feng Shui House Book* by Gina Lazenby.
  Demystifies feng shui and explains how it can bring
  harmony to the home.
- *Paint: The Big Book of Natural Color* by Elizabeth
  Hilliard and Stafford Cliff. Takes a fresh approach to
  using color in the home.
- *Mood Indigo: Decorating with Rich, Dark Colors* by
  Vinny Lee. The definitive guide to using an
  adventurous design palette in the home.
- *Coming Home: Spiritual Interiors* by Vinny Lee.
  Finding peace and comfort in you living space.

Picture Credits

Cover Image: Tim Goffe
Elizabeth Whiting and Associates: Pages vi, 4, 6, 6, 7, 7,
9, 10, 12, 14, 19, 19, 21, 23, 31, 35, 41, 43, 44, 47, 49, 51,
53, 61, 67, 68, 74, 78, 81, 87, 89
Red Cover: pages 3, 26, 27, 36, 63, 63

Robert Harding: pages 19, 24, 26, 26, 32, 63, 65, 70, 76
Getty Stone Images: pages 39, 72, 73, 83
Andrea Jones Location Photography: Page 57
Garden Picture Library: Page 58
Richard Croft Photography: Page 75
Anthony Blake Photo Library: Page 84